D1347023

WOULD YOU WANT TO LIVE HERE?

Alison Hawes

Published 2009 by
A & C Black Publishers Ltd.
36 Soho Square, London, W1D 3QY
www.acblack.com

ISBN HB 978-1-4081-0957-1
PB 978-1-4081-1284-7

Series consultant: Gill Matthews
Text copyright © 2009 Alison Hawes

A CIP catalogue for this book is available from the British Library.

This book is produced using paper that is made from wood grown in managed,
sustainable forests. It is natural, renewable and recyclable. The logging and
manufacturing processes conform to the environmental regulations
of the country of origin.

Produced for A & C Black by Calcium.
Printed and bound in China by C&C Offset Printing Co.

All the internet addresses given in this book were correct at the time of going to
press. The author and publishers regret any inconvenience caused if addresses
have changed or sites have ceased to exist, but can accept no responsibility for
any such changes.

Acknowledgements

The publishers would like to thank the following for their kind permission
to reproduce their photographs:
Cover: Corbis: Dean Conger; Shutterstock: Vladimir Melnik.
Pages: Alamy Images: Mediscan/Medical-on-Line 7; Corbis: Dean Conger
6, EPA 10, EPA/Wu Hong 15; Dreamstime: Totorean 13r; Getty Images:
DigitalGlobe 16; Istockphoto: Juergen Sack 19, Joris Van 12, William
Walsh 18; Photolibrary: Oxford Scientific/Ariadne Van Zandbergen 9;
Rex Features: Richard Jones 14, K Nomach 8; Shutterstock: Robert
Paul van Beets 5, Marcus Brown 21, Franck Camhi 20, Jules Kitano
13l, Terry Poche 17, Jerry Sharp 4, Sia Chen How 11.

CONTENTS

LIVING AT EXTREMES

Where do you live? Can you find it on this map?
Many people live in homes and places that
are very different from yours.

**Floods occur in parts of
the world where rain falls
heavily and suddenly.**

DID YOU KNOW?

The people who live in the
places marked on this map
live in some of the **harshest
environments** on Earth.

The driest
inhabited
place on Earth

Atacama Desert

Earthquakes happen in the places on the map shaded blue.

The hottest inhabited place on Earth

The coldest inhabited place on Earth

Oymyakon

Linfen

The most polluted inhabited place on Earth

Mawsynram

Dallol Depression

The wettest inhabited place on Earth

Tristan da Cunha

The most remote inhabited place on Earth

THE COLDEST PLACE ON EARTH

Oymyakon is a small village in Russia. The temperature in Oymyakon can be three times as cold as your freezer! Oymyakon is the coldest inhabited place on Earth.

The temperature in Oymyakon is often –50°C (–58°F), or lower!

The houses in Oymyakon have steep roofs to keep out the snow.

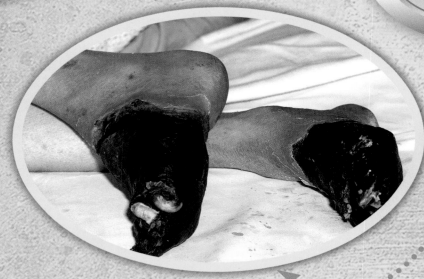

I DON'T BELIEVE IT!
Even when it is
−50°C (−58°F)
the river in the
village does
not freeze!

Frostbite **has made
many people here
lose fingers
and toes.**

TOO COLD TO FARM

The ground is too cold and hard to grow much food. So, villagers mostly live on horse and reindeer meat.

AMAZING

When it is −50°C:

Mobile phones do not work

Pens do not work

Diesel fuel freezes

7

THE HOTTEST PLACE ON EARTH

The Dallol **Depression**, in Africa, is a place of rocks, volcanoes, and **salt flats**. The Afar people live here. They are called **nomads**.

The Dallol Depression is the hottest inhabited place on Earth.

90°
80°
70°
60°
50°
40°
30°
20°
10°
0°

The temperature in the Dallol Depression is often 34°C (94°F).

THE WORKING DAY

The Afar women walk miles every day to find water. The Afar men cut and sell the salt from the salt flats.

I DON'T BELIEVE IT!

The Afar women cover hot springs with rocks. The steam from the springs, cools on the rocks. This turns back into water. The women collect this water to drink.

The Afar people live in huts made from palm mats and sticks. They can be folded up when the people move.

The Afar people live on meat, milk, and cheese from their goats.

THE WETTEST PLACE ON EARTH

Mawsynram is a small village in India. More rain falls here in one day than falls in some places in one year! It is the wettest inhabited place on Earth.

DID YOU KNOW?

A knup is a waterproof covering shaped like a giant shell. It is worn by people in Mawsynram to keep them dry as they work in the rain.

This man is wearing a knup as he picks crops in a field.

Rice plants need a lot of water to grow. Lots of rice is grown in Mawsynram!

12m
11m
10m
9m
8m
7m
6m
5m
4m
3m
2m
1m

Mawsynram has almost 12 m (42 ft) of rain in a year.

MONSOON WEATHER

On **monsoon** days, the villagers may have to change their wet clothes many times.

THE DRIEST PLACE ON EARTH

The Atacama **Desert** in Chile is a place of sand, dust, and rocks. It has not rained in some parts of the Atacama for over 400 years!

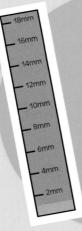

The Atacama has about one millimetre only of rain a year.

The Atacama desert is the driest place on Earth.

DESERT HOMES

Some people live in **oasis** villages in the middle of the desert.

San Pedro is an oasis village built with adobe bricks. Adobe bricks keep the houses cool.

Big pipes carry water to towns in the desert.

I DON'T BELIEVE IT!

Some villagers put up nets to catch the fog. The fog drips into pipes, which take the water to the village.

DID YOU KNOW?

Mummies of people who lived thousands of years ago have been found in the Atacama Desert.

THE MOST POLLUTED PLACE ON EARTH

Linfen is a big city in China. The air in Linfen is often filled with thick, black dust.

DID YOU KNOW?

Many people in Linfen have breathing problems because of the pollution.

Linfen is one of the most polluted cities on Earth.

FUEL

Coal is a very important fuel in China. The dust and **smog** come from the coal mines and factories in and around Linfen.

People in Linfen often wear face masks when they go out.

GOOD NEWS!

Some polluting factories in Linfen are being shut down.

I DON'T BELIEVE IT!

Linfen is so polluted you cannot see the stars at night.

THE MOST REMOTE PLACE ON EARTH

Tristan da Cunha is an island in the Atlantic. Its nearest neighbours are more than 16,000 km (1,000 miles) away! Tristan da Cunha is the most remote place on Earth.

I DON'T BELIEVE IT!
The islanders finally got television in 2001, but they only have one channel.

This aerial photograph of Tristan da Cunha was taken from above.

ISLAND LIFE

About 270 people live on the island. They sell stamps and crayfish to people overseas to make a living. The post takes a long time to arrive and there is no way to get to hospital quickly.

Crayfish live in the waters around the island.

DID YOU KNOW?

The islanders share
• one school
• one policeman
• one doctor
• one swimming pool
• and eight surnames between them!

LIVING IN AN EARTHQUAKE ZONE

Big earthquakes can be dangerous.
Many people live in places
where big earthquakes happen.

**Earthquakes happen
when the Earth's
crust moves.**

**I DON'T
BELIEVE IT!**
There is an
earthquake in the
world about every
11 seconds!

KILLER QUAKE!

Big earthquakes can destroy homes and kill people. People in earthquake zones have to try to keep themselves safe.

Some people try to build earthquake-proof homes.

19

LIVING IN A FLOOD ZONE

Rivers and seas sometimes
flood. Too much water
can be dangerous.
Big floods can destroy
homes and kill people.

DANGER

Floods can also destroy
- crops and animals
- roads and bridges
- power lines
- factories and shops

**This dam stops the
River Nile flooding
every year.**

FLOOD ZONES

Some people in flood zones build homes that will not wash away in a flood.

DID YOU KNOW?

Waste is often caught up in flood water. Diseases can be caught by drinking the dirty water.

This house is built on stilts to keep it above a flood.

GLOSSARY

adobe sun-dried clay or mud bricks

crust the top layer of the Earth's surface

depression a low-lying area of land

desert a dry area of land that has little rain

environment the conditions of the world
around you

frostbite when parts of the body are injured
by extreme cold

harsh very difficult. A place that is very difficult
to live in is often described as harsh

inhabited a place in which people live

monsoon a wind that brings very heavy rain

mummy a body that has been treated so it will
not decay quickly

nomads people who move from place to place

oasis a place in a desert where water is found

salt flats dried-up saltwater lakes

smog mixture of fog and smoke

FURTHER INFORMATION

Websites

Find out about homes around the world at:
www.ict.mic.ul.ie/websites/2002/Imelda_Fitzgerald/index.htm

Click on to guides to earthquakes, floods, or extreme weather at:
http://news.bbc.co.uk/cbbcnews/hi/find_out/guides/default.stm

Find out about weather, people, and homes at:
**www.bbc.co.uk/schools/whatisweather/weatherandpeople/
    index.shtml**

Books

Homes Around the World by Nicky Barber. Wayland (2006)

Shattering Earthquakes by Louise Spilsbury. Heinemann (2004)

Violent Volcanoes by Louise Spilsbury. Heinemann (2004)

INDEX